FROM THE PROJECTS...

TO THE PROJECTS

My Road to Success

ABIDAN PADILLA

From the Projects… to the Projects

Copyright © 2020 Abidan Padilla

ISBN: 978-1-61170-303-0

All rights reserved. No part of this publication may be reproduced, stored in a retrieval system or transmitted in any form or by any means, electronic, mechanical, photocopies, recording or otherwise, without the prior written consent of the author, except in the case of brief quotations embodied in critical reviews.

To contact the author: apconstructiontraining@gmail.com

Abidan would like to thank the following people for their help with this book:
    All photographs: Alma C. Padilla
    1st draft editing: Stephanie J. Padilla
    2nd draft editing: Abidan Austin Padilla jr.
    Final editing & book design: Thomas Proctor
    Graphic design (book cover): Gabriel Moreno

Published by:

Robertson Publishing™
www.RobertsonPublishing.com

Printed in the USA and UK on acid-free paper.

To purchase additional books go to:
www.apconstructiontraining.com *or* Amazon.com.

Dedication

I would like to give a special thank you to my beautiful wife Alma C. Padilla for her bravery, persistence and for never giving up on me throughout our 24 years of marriage.

Alma is a strong women, my wife and friend. She has been our family's backbone and has kept us unified despite the tough circumstances we faced.

Everyday I appreciate her for her support and for playing a major role in my transformation into the person I am today.

Alma and Abidan

Wisdom is born from trials and errors;

And so failure has been my strength and success.

Abidan Padilla

TABLE OF CONTENTS

Foreword 1

Chapter 1 - The Projects 3

Chapter 2 - Turning Point 7

Chapter 3 - High School 11

Chapter 4 - The L.A. Riots 14

Chapter 5 - Gangs / Drugs 18

Chapter 6 - Graduation 26

Chapter 7 - Marriage 30

Chapter 8 - Daughter 35

Chapter 9 - Taste of Success 40

Chapter 10 - Son 46

Chapter 11 - Family Loss 51

Chapter 12 - Personal Goals 55

Chapter 13 - Coaching Sports 59

Chapter 14 - Business Owners 63

Chapter 15 - Real Estate Investments 67

Chapter 16 - Persistence Through Recession 71

Chapter 17 - New Contract 74

Invitation & Challenge 77

The Padilla Family 79

New Personal Goals — Stephanie, Austin 81

Ways to Turn Desires Into Gold 83

Abidan's Personal Goals and Prayer 84

Foreword

The idea of a ten-year-old boy living in Watts, California, having the fortitude and strength to even *survive* the violence and crime that permeated the entire east Los Angeles area in the '80s stretches our imagination.

The first massive Watts riots in the '60s set the ground rules for violence. My wife and I lived in Hollywood in those times, when horrified residents watched TV reports of angry Watts residents standing on the blocked-off freeways and firing guns at the incoming airline planes trying to land at the airport. After several near-hits, the aircraft routes were re-routed out over the ocean. The L.A. freeways were mostly avoided.

In those twenty years leading into the '80s, very little improvements in conditions were evident for the area, and residency was still a risky venture. In Watts, jobs were scarce and money even more so. Survival was the keyword, and that many times meant that Watts youth had no choice but to join neighborhood gangs for protection.

Gang life was treacherous. Acquiring money was the only way to either leave the area or simply exist. Fighting was constant, with the accompanying knifings and gunshot deaths from warring gangs, as well as the always dangerous pursuing Police. During the frequent riots, looting was standard procedure. During this entire period, stealing and re-selling cars became a matter-of-fact business for the gangs, who even calculated what time in prison might bring in considering a possible crime. This was a way of thinking that differed from the norm, all driven by the need for money to escape.

In the midst of all this emerged a highly-motivated and determined young man, *Abidan Padilla*. He survived daily fighting in gang warfare and intimidation, prison and jail, and even being almost killed from being shot in the back, with a lengthy recovery.

The vicious society which surrounded Abidan and pulled on him like a dark magnet was not able to deter him from his dedication to achieving success and wealth as he kept on his path.

Then two things happened which convinced Abidan to finally leave the danger of the hoodlum environment.

The first was a chance meeting with a beautiful young woman named Alma, with whom Abidan immediately fell in love at first sight. Although it took a year for them to get together, instant responsibility became a priority matched with his drive. After their marriage, their two families struggled together to get through the terrible pressure and danger of the constant Watts crime exposure.

The second was the shooting and ultimate death of his older brother, *shot seven times in the back* and electrifying each member of both families, requiring enormous efforts working together to get through the tragedy and its aftermath.

What happens next is an incredible series of events, all driven by Abidan's unstoppable goal pursuits and growing power on a straight line for success.

Abidan and his family's story has deeply affected me and has changed my attitude toward life. I find myself closely watching for opportunities that match my true interests and loves. I realize now that I can *only* attain the things I want for the rest of my life if I indeed *totally believe in acquiring them*.

This is a *spectacular* story.

Thomas C. Procter

Chapter 1

The Projects

*The daily innocence of a kid becomes
a daily survival tactic.*

I was ten years old. We were living in the rough Willow Brook area of the City of Compton. My father was working in a metal and copper salvage shop in South Central Los Angeles, working vigorously to make the monthly rent and put food on the table. My mother had to be a strong woman, especially living in her hard and unstable surroundings. She worked various jobs for a few years but having two girls and four boys she was destined to become a homemaker to attend to all of her kids.

That summer my parents decided to move into the Nickerson Gardens Housing Projects because the monthly rent was more reasonable and the living space was exactly what they were looking for: 4 bedrooms, 1 bath, a living room, and a kitchen. The boys shared a room with bunk beds. My Grandma and my younger sister also had shared their room, while my older sister had her own, as well as my parents.

Moving into the projects was extremely intense. It was a predominantly black community, and I felt like everyone was staring at us, wondering who all these crazy Mexicans were. After a few days of looking out our windows, we made our first attempt to play outside hoping to go unnoticed. But that didn't work. We were approached by a few kids who started to question us and ask *what set we claim* such as, "Where you from, Blood?" That continued for the entire summer and then back to school we went.

My older brother and older sister attended Edison Jr. High, while the rest of us attended Parmelee Elementary on 76th Street and Hooper Avenue. Every day my mother would drive my father to work at 6 a.m., and then drive a few more miles into South Central to drop us off at our sitter's house. Our parents decided to get a sitter so that our mother would not have to make the trip twice. We wait for a couple of hours at our sitters house, then at 8:00 a.m we would walk to school. That was our daily morning routine until I graduated from elementary school in 1988.

Nickerson Garden Projects 1986
Abidan on the right next to his younger siblings.

Four young brothers growing up in Compton, California, 1984. Abidan 2nd from the right.

My parents decided it was time to register us to the nearest middle school in Watts, which was Markham Middle School on 104th Street and Compton Avenue. This didn't work out, because there were local gangs who bullied all kids, including us when we first arrived.

I was now twelve years old, walking to school with two of my brothers and a couple of Hispanic kids who just moved into the projects earlier that summer.

I remember one day, early in the morning, we all met up to walk to school and several other groups of gangs were also walking towards the school. Again they asked us, "where you from?" and a fight ensued. Pushing and shoving went on for several minutes between two or three groups of gangs, but luckily, we were able to escape without any injuries. After school, we encountered the same aggression from another group of local gangs.

From there the story changes. For everyone. I was forced to evolve: From a kid who was a straight-A student to a toughened gang member on survival mode and determined to follow my lifelong rush to self-success. Later, I realized this decision was the start of my already established drive to succeed in a mostly hostile society at the time, despite all of the obstacles in my path.

Despite the constant on-going violence and personal danger, I continued to attend Markham for the rest of that school year. I then requested to get transferred to Edison Middle School in South Central where most of the kids with whom I went to elementary school were attending. Eventually, my mother decided she would transfer me even if it meant getting up earlier to drive across town.

But the issues did not end there. We still had to drive in and out of the projects daily. We lived near the intersection of East 115th Street and Success Avenue, just north of the soon-to-be-built 105 freeway.

After a couple of years of living in the projects, we met a few neighbors that genuinely welcomed us in. One of them was an older, well-respected Blood. He was completely cool with my father. He and his wife would even take my younger brother to the Forum to watch boxing matches.

Chapter 2

Turning Point

Don't allow yourself to be easily influenced.

Several other fights broke out throughout the rest of the school year, but things were starting to change. Maybe even ease up. The racial tension was no joke. African-American communities had dominated the local schools for years.

Just before graduating, my father continued to work endless hours, however $2-$3 dollars per hour was just not getting the job done. We were a family full of several boys wanting the latest and greatest style of wardrobe, such as *FILA* Shoes, *Chuck Taylors*, and not sure if you remember the infamous *Pumas*.

My father never gave up and had some entrepreneurial thoughts that caught my interest. Early one Saturday morning he suggested that we open up a candy store. I had no objections.

I was the first one to arrive each day, as I was eager to sell all the soda pops and candy all the same day. After the word of mouth advertisement got around, I sold about 50 dollars worth of candy in one week and was able to buy my first pair of *FILA's*. My brothers saw that and then quickly wanted to be a part of the candy store. So we alternated shifts weekly.

I tried to think of other ways to make money, but nothing was popping into my head. I was low on cash, and after three weeks of waiting for the candy store rotation to get back to me, I went broke.

I remember going to the Hollywood horse track as kids with my parents, We loved feeding apples to the horses while my parents would wager bets on their favorite horses. One day was very memorable because I got the chance to meet *Laffit Pincay Jr.* and *Bill Shoemaker* as they ran around the park.

I later thought we might make some money if we sold sodas at the horse track. One thing led to another, and next thing you know we were selling beers; and I will tell you it was better than selling candy. There was always big crowd at the track. We would walk among the crowd pulling our beer coolers until we found places where we could set up, and then we'd sell right out of the coolers. We did this until the crowd thinned and then we would move to a new place and set up again. We were going home with about a $300 profit each day. This happened right before I started middle school.

NWA Straight Outta Compton album was released in 1988, the same year *Kirk Gibson* hit the Game One World Series home run in October. I remember like it was yesterday. I was excited about the new clothes I was going to wear to school on my first day and listening to the song "Dopeman" by *NWA*.

The following September I attended Edison Jr. High. I was in the 8th grade, and I started to hang out with some of my former elementary school friends who were gang banging at the time. I thought to myself, *No, I'm not getting into that lifestyle.* Yet with the daily tension, it seemed like it was almost forced upon me. Kindness was non-existent. It almost felt like everyone had something to prove, whether it was to be the so-called "Machismo," or just not wanting to be perceived as weak.

During the school year, I kept to myself most of the time, while my older brother, who was in the 9th grade, was hanging out at the "Wall." If you were one of the guys hanging out at the wall you were pretty much in and/or accepted as far as basic requirements for gangs went.

Los Angeles in 1988. Abidan is standing second from right, in between two of his brothers.

My younger brother had just started the 7th grade, and one morning during school a local gang went around picking fights. We were fed up with all the bullshit, so we fought back. My older brother and the other "wall guys" happened to be at the wall during the incident. Once they saw what was going on, a bigger and more brutal fight broke out and it lasted for what seemed like hours. We used knives and "knuckles," and only a few of us escaped without cuts or broken bones.

The following year, I started going out more without my parents' consent, my grades started dropping rapidly, and I rarely found myself home for dinner. Later that summer of 1989, I joined a gang. I thought it was the best decision I could make to combat all the opposition and rivalry going on.

I fought. That was the only way I found to get through my junior high school years. It was tough, but I did it. And now it was behind me.

My parents were happy that I graduated from junior high school. It was a great accomplishment for all of us at that time. However, I knew big changes were about to be made. It felt like we were growing up at a blurred and incomprehensible speed. A "you're on your own" kind of feeling in a hostile environment.

After I graduated from Edison Jr High, I knew the real test ahead of me was going to be my move into high school. This was to be the real challenge. I thought to myself, *Am I going to be easily influenced and overcome by gangs?* And, *how am I going to make it through this very critical age of my life?"*

Our elementary school mantra, "feeling strong looking great, we're the class of 88!" We were proud to graduate and move on to Middle School. Now, moving from middle school to high school I wasn't too sure the feeling was going to be the same.

* * * * *

Most L.A. communities were predominantly African American throughout the '70-'80s. When the '90s came around, the American-Hispanic population grew in numbers so rapidly that it triggered concern and extensive retaliatory violence throughout Compton, Watts, and South Central. And it was all over "Territory."

Chapter 3

High School

The most memorable days of my life, that I never got to enjoy.

Summertime came around, and the streets were hotter than "July," if you know what I mean. Every day you would see several cops out on patrol. You would also see every street corner full of *activities* such as people drinking, smoking, gambling-rolling dice, listening to the old cassettes playing boomboxes, partying. And fighting. Always fighting. Sounds chaotic, I know, but after a few years of living in the projects it was normal for us.

Summer came to an end, and the next thing I knew it was my first day at Fremont High School in 1991. Enrollment seemed like it was taking forever. Fremont High was predominantly Hispanic, with multiple gang members in and around the area. It was no surprise that I somehow found myself in one. It was violent. Multiple riots were breaking out throughout the entire school. I was personally involved in a couple of fights which ultimately led to my suspension, and about one month later I ended up getting expelled.

My parents were extremely disappointed, but at the time I just did not care. I felt like a true "G," so I continued my gang activities. My father quickly enrolled me into Southgate High the following week to try to help me get back on track. I knew my parents were desperate.

Deep inside my heart I wanted to stay out of trouble, but on the first day at Southgate, I found myself in a fight with multiple gang members from the school. The counselor called my father to pick me up immediately. It was clear that Southgate did not want me back.

For the next few months, through the holidays, I didn't know what I was doing with my life. I felt like I had failed and let my family down. All I could do was try to get back into a school, but no one wanted to accept me. My grades had dropped dramatically, due to my poor choices, and there was no one to blame but myself.

I continued to hang out with my homeboys and began to consume drugs and alcohol. I thought that I was cool, and no one could get in the way of my endeavors. At the time, I felt like I finally had it all figured out. My parents were upset, but I enjoyed being a part of something that didn't have a retirement plan or a pension at the end. Don't get me wrong, I enjoyed my teenage/young adult years, but looking back I just wish I could have made better decisions.

As the year came to an end, I remember the candy store was not bringing in enough revenue, or I just evolved through it. Maybe my spending habits outgrew the candy store revenue.

At this point, the crack epidemic was going around the Ghettos, and more arrests were going on daily throughout South Central Los Angeles. The gang units were in place and doors were flying off their hinges from the battering rams.

Living in the projects throughout this long of a period was unheard of for a Hispanic family and my father wasn't ready to move away just yet. For the next few months, we had several encounters with our neighbors that involved guns and cops. We were kids you did not want to mess with, and everyone in the projects knew that. For being the only Hispanics in the projects, it was cool to feel respected by your neighbors. The success of our apartment on East 115 Street will always be remembered for its persistence, survival, and respect *by* all and *for* all.

New Years Eve arrived and the sky was lit up like the 4th of July, but no fireworks were used. It was gunfire play of all kinds. Now ask yourself, do you want *that* for your life or for your kids? It was becoming clearer: *Get an education so you won't have to experience that lifestyle. Let's make our future generations better.*

It was an unsettled and perturbed time in the projects, waiting on the Rodney King verdict that would soon to be revealed.

Chapter 4

THE L.A. RIOTS

A critical moment that changed everything.

1991 came and went; I was still trying to figure out how to make money. I wasn't going to school, and sitting at home was not working out for me. I started hanging out more frequently with a good friend, who I later found out was living across the street from the projects.

Late evenings I would go over to his house and we would listen to DJ Quick and smoke some weed. That was my thing to do since I was not going to school. However, it still didn't feel as if I was being productive. I wasn't, because I wasn't making money.

Around this time, The Rodney King Trial was going on and L.A. was energized with lots of emotions. It was a vivid memory; walking home bent over through the projects, dodging gunshots as they rang off. People were running as if the world was ending. As the sun went down and night came around, the entire city was burning, and smoke from the huge fires filled the sky.

In the middle of it all, we looted the popular stores in those days such as Newberry's, Pic & Save, and a few others. That went on for three days and three nights before the national guard rolled into town in their armored vehicles, guns at the ready, shields up, and clothed in bullet-proof vests. They closed off streets, fired tear gas, and did heavy face-to-face confrontations with anyone that stood before them, generally crunching them to the ground. They handcuffed bloodied unlucky ones and dragged them into their wagons, then to jail. People were driving off with their car trunks full of new clothes, new shoes, and food.

We thought we made out when in reality it was all a risk for nothing. Several people died during those three days and our communities were burned down to ashes.

Following the L.A. riots in April of 1992, I continued my hood-banging activities. I felt like I was unstoppable. One late Saturday night, I met with my friends at our regular hangout and the partying went on for hours. As we partied a car pulled up and someone shouted out my name. It was an older homeboy.

"Abidan!" He was excited. "Your uncle is getting jumped at the park. Get in!"

I jumped into the car and we raced to the park. Shortly after arriving, shots were being fired towards us and we dove into the floor of the car. Then everyone in the car fired a huge volley of shots back and we barrelled out of there at high speed with bullets zipping by us.

After blowing through a couple of red lights, we were pulled over by the cops near Florence and Miramonte, and I was arrested. Although no one was hurt, I was charged with two counts of assault with a deadly weapon. I went to Los Padrinos Juvenile Hall for the first time in my life, and I'll tell you this: if you *don't* want to be successful that place might be perfect for you. It has "No Future" written all over it. Good luck if you think that way. You're going to need it.

I didn't quite understand what had transpired, but I was smart enough to know that my life was on a roller coaster and it was moving downhill fast.

At Los Padrinos I was given a bible. I read it every night before going to sleep and found the stories were very interesting. I enjoyed Moses's journey through the desert because Moses never gave up on searching for the destination that Jesus wanted him to find for the people. Once he reached the destination *he died*. He didn't even get to see it. That is what you call unselfish faith for others.

After about four weeks of trial, I was sentenced to one year at Camp Holton. The camp wasn't a walk in the park either for a fifteen-year-old kid, but I found the courage to suck it up and fight through it, and I mean *fight* through it. I fought several times in LP, Sylmar, and Camp Holton. I also managed to figure out a way where I could fight and get away with it. Otherwise, I would end up in solitary confinement better known as the "Hole".

For the fighting we would meet behind the main building and place others on the track behind the buildings to watch for employees that might see the fighting going on. If the spotters observed anyone coming onto the scene, they would alert those fighting, allowing them to get away without being caught.

After multiple fights, I was finally left alone. I was given respect by all inmates and I continued towards meeting my goals, which were at that time getting the hell out of there. It was such a waste of time and energy and *I was not making any money.*

In the fall of '92, my father and mother drove up to visit me and broke the worst news to me at that time. They told me my second oldest brother had been shot seven times while partying on the weekend. He was in a coma for several days and it appeared that he might not make it through. I was furious and wanted to go AWOL, but that wouldn't have changed anything.

We chose this lifestyle and we knew it came with big consequences.

The following year my parents brought him up to visit me. He was doing a lot better but had lost a lot of weight. I couldn't believe the stress we were putting on our parents, but in the hood that was called "survival."

Abidan on the public pay phone in South Central Los Angeles. 1992

Chapter 5

Gangs / Drugs

The decisions you make today will forever impact your life.

Just before my release from Camp Holton, the staff put together an event for Valentine's Day. All the qualified inmates would be allowed to invite their parents to come up to visit and enjoy a small concert in which Brenton Woods was performing. That event was good, and we even had Mrs. Gloria Molina from the L.A. County Board of Supervisors attended. Mrs. Molina took me aside and we sat on a bench together.

"Abidan," she asked softly, "what are you doing here?"

That seemed like a strange question.

"Well, Mrs. Molina," I replied, "I guess I got in trouble with the police. I ended up in here."

"Do you like it here?"

"No."

"Then *why* are you here?"

"Because I broke a bunch of laws and got caught."

"Abidan." She leaned closer. "I'm asking you *why* you are here. I *know* you have been breaking laws." She gestured at the facility around them. "This is a dead-end." She looked up at the sky as if to find the right words. "Abidan, I've been watching you for a long time. You seem to be different than the other hoodlums that live here and are constantly in trouble with the law. I've noticed you have, at times, demonstrated some type of unusual drive which seems different than the run-of-the-mill gang bangers. Can you explain that?"

"Mrs. Molina, from the time I was ten years old I've always wanted to make money. A lot of it. I've always wanted to be successful. And I've believed that *getting* a lot of money will be my ticket out of here."

"And your fighting? Why are you always fighting?"

"I fight anything and anybody who stands in my way and tries to keep me from my goals."

"Look," she smiled easily. "You have a supportive family. You have my support. You are still young and can do something about your life."

She stood so I stood too.

"I have to get back to the group now." Taking my hand in hers and searching my eyes, she said, "Abidan, stay focused. It's time for you to *get it together.*"

I thanked her for her positive support that day! I could feel it as she walked away.

I was finally released from the camp.

Driving back home to the Nickerson Gardens Projects with my father felt so unreal. It felt like *waking up from a dream and it's still a dream,* or something like that. But the ride home was silent and panoramic. I took deep breaths.

As soon as I arrived home, I hugged everyone and went up to my room to lay down. I was still trying to process what just happened and how I was going to adjust back into my new daily social activities. It wasn't too long before my homeboys knew I was out. They came by to pick me up and I simply went back out to the streets. *So much for trying to figure out how to get back into society.*

In some odd way, I felt good about being recognized by everyone for the way I handled myself while at Camp Holton. It seemed like everyone knew what went on in there and were waiting to ask me questions like, "How many fights did you have?" "What camps did you go to?" "Did you like it?"

People would even tell me that if I liked being incarcerated, I must be insane. Of course, *I didn't like it,* but because of the way I chose to live my life I often found myself there.

Four brothers growing up in Gangland.

Later that summer of 1993, I enrolled back into school at the CDC High School in Los Angeles. The school was established by a couple of local judges, Mr. Moore and Mr. Jones. I owe them a lot of gratitude for having given me the opportunity to get back into school, and for dealing with such a tough crowd that had lots of push-back for no apparent reason. I'll explain later in this chapter.

CDC High was within walking distance from Fremont High, the school I attended for about a month before I got expelled. It was the middle of the week and we got out at noon. I decided to walk to Fremont high and knew I would arrive right after school let out. Once I arrived, I nonchalantly climbed over the fence and met up with a few friends, as if that was the normal way I might visit this campus. We then proceeded walking around campus talking to everyone who I had not seen in over a year.

* * * * *

Several high school girls were walking together, talking about things that high school girls talk about. Looking up, one of the girls suddenly found a tall young man in her path.

"*Hmmm,*" she thought, *"he's kinda cute. I wonder what he's all about? Maybe he'll want to talk some."*

* * * * *

I suddenly found myself walking right in the direction of a beautiful looking lady who was also walking, with her friends, *directly toward me.*

We made eye contact and stopped, facing each other a few feet apart. She smiled and my heart melted into my shoes. I was beyond awkward.

"Hi, I – uh." I actually shuffled my feet like an eight-year-old and felt redness flowing into my face and neck.

"Uh," is all I could croak out. *What is wrong with me?*

"Uh, I, uh, what's your name?" I finally blurted out.

Her voice was melodic.

"Alma."

I instantly felt her name riding on the tip of an arrow embedding itself within my heart, which at this moment was pounding furiously as if trying to jump out of my body. Something told me this was a permanent thing.

I didn't have a pick-up line, and I didn't feel like laying some insulting effort on her. She was *quality.* I found myself stumbling over words that wouldn't come out, as if trying to talk with a shoe in my mouth. *What am I going to do?*

Alma smiled, noticing my awkwardness.

"Do you have one too?" she asked gently.

I gulped noticeably.

"One *what?*"

"*Name,*" she replied with a flavor of coyness. "Most people I talk to have one."

"Oh!" I was relieved. "My name is Abidan. A-bi-dan," I repeated as if this might permanently embed the memory in her beautiful brain.

Alma extended her hand and looked up into my eyes.

"Hi, Abidan. Nice to meet you. Do you go to school here? I don't think I've ever seen you on campus."

I grabbed her hand as gently as I could, resisting the almost overpowering desire to kiss it finger by finger and pull her close to me. *Where is my White Stallion when I need him!*

"Uh, no. I don't. I'm just visiting the campus. To see old friends, you know."

"Has it been successful?"

"Oh, yeah!" I was totally distracted. "It has. I've seen guys I haven't seen in a year or more. Yep. It's been good seeing them all again."

"Do you live nearby?"

Impossible! Am I really making progress with this unbelievable girl?

"Yeah. Yes," I corrected, trying desperately to control my madly-beating heart which I was sure she could see forcing my shirt to bounce. "Not too far away." I motioned vaguely off-campus. "Over in that direction."

"Are you a student somewhere?"

Uh oh. How do I explain my situation?

"Well, yes," I scrambled to remain calm. "I'm attending a specialty school."

Oh, please don't ask about more details.

Feeling a bit more confident, I finally mustered up the will to get into small talk, and as our friends moved away to leave us alone, we talked for a while. I found out later that one of the first characteristics she saw in me was as a protector. That was a big surprise that only added to my interest in her.

I couldn't wait any longer.

"Uh, Alma." I took a deep breath.

"Yes?"

"Would you possibly consider giving me your phone number? I would love to talk with you more."

She looked so calm as she smiled. I held my breath.

"Yes, I would like that. And you can give me yours."

A heavenly choir of angels was singing The "Halleluiah Chorus" in the background.

After we exchanged numbers, I held her hand again.

"You will call me?" I asked gingerly.

"No. You will have to call me. Good girls don't call guys."

That did it. From that moment on I wanted this beautiful girl in my life.

Despite my nervousness, I still managed to get her phone number that day. *But I did not speak with her for a year after that.*

* * * * *

For the next year, I continued my street-banging ways, such as hanging out, smoking drugs, stealing cars, etc.

I would *continue* on this reckless path while continuing at CDC School. CDC stands for "Central Detention Center." If you miss school, you go directly back to jail, and jail was one thing I did not want. This is the way their psychology worked. *And yet I still continued, not sure why.*

One afternoon during school we were outside for lunch and I was sitting on the lunch bench. I was feeling kind of nauseous so I rested my head on the table. Later I was awakened by paramedics who told me I had a seizure and needed to go to the hospital for medical evaluation. I was moving faster than my internal system could handle, causing seizure attacks.

Later that year, in '93, *I was shot in the back by a drug cartel.*

The cartel was extremely upset that I had been breaking in at all its dope spots and taking its drugs and money. They knew who I was and would follow me daily until their opportunity to get to me came up. Their opportunity did come up and they cornered and shot me.

I managed to survive a gunshot to my lower back. It was a through-and-through shot, which means it did not impact any organs. They say a cat lives nine lives. Well, I sure felt like a lucky cat that day.

Recovering from the gunshot, I decided to stop drinking and smoking drugs to better my health. So for the next year or so I recovered and detoxed and stayed sober.

One day as I was picking up my younger brother from Fremont High I saw my beautiful Alma walking on the street with some of her friends. I was with my parents, sitting in the backseat of my dad's 1983 Oldsmobile Cutlass, and she smiled and waved as we drove past. I almost broke my neck looking at her as we went by.

Later that evening I vigorously searched for her number for hours, "*I know I have it,*" I said to myself. After several excruciating hours of looking, I finally found it in the back of my steel locker written with a sharpie, the same place I placed it a year earlier. I remember disposing of the original paper copy. *No wonder I couldn't find it...*

The moment of truth came when I called her, and her sister answered as if they knew I was going to call. I was nervous and excited. When Alma came to the phone it was like we knew we were going to talk for a while. We talked and talked. We both fell asleep on the phone. When I woke up the next morning the telephone cord was around my neck choking me, making me think I was in an MMA rear neck hold.

Ha. It felt good speaking with her, and I couldn't get enough. So I called her again, but this time her mother answered and told me she had a time limit.

Oops! We adjusted.

Alma and Abidan attending Fremont High School.

Chapter 6

Graduation

An uncertain future with a great passion for success.

1994 arrived as if it were trying to push 1993 into a distant memory as quickly as possible. I bought my first car from an auction, a 1987 cutlass, and it cost me $500. It needed a lot of touch-ups; everything from the interior to the engine, and a paint job. But I was excited about my new car.

About one week after I purchased the Cutlass, my 19-year-old older brother made me an offer. He said that he would trade me his 1987 four-door Chevy Caprice that had a sound system if I would give him the Cutlass and $1500. I didn't think about it too much and went for it. I just wanted to start driving a car and wanted to go out with my new girlfriend.

I was in love, but I didn't have a job to take my girlfriend out. I wanted to take her to the movies or to go eat a good dinner, but I couldn't.

However, she would take *me* out, and occasionally she'd treat me to dinner. It was nice but I felt it was wrong. So I continued my criminal activities to rake in some money.

By this time the local project gangs knew who we were and didn't bother us at all. I used the parking lot as a parking station for all the stolen vehicles, known as "Grand Theft Auto's" (GTA's). I'd sell these vehicles to the highest bidder. It was a strong market for new and used cars.

My negotiation skills were improving every day, and you could say I was "employee of the month", or something along those lines, because I was on the go! One weekend, I remember picking up six cars to be exact, and I sold them all that same weekend, at an average of $500 per vehicle. *Movie dates and popcorn weren't going to be an issue any longer.*

I continued this pattern for the next year or so, and although I'd gotten lucky, it was just a matter a time before my luck ran out.

It was a Saturday morning and I was drinking my coffee when my ride showed up. It was time to go to work. I didn't have to do this because I had about $900 in my pocket. However, I felt it was necessary to meet my weekly quota. Maybe it just became an addiction to a false promise of evil wealth.

We drove up to a parking lot of one of the most popular malls in Los Angeles. We started our surveillance for incoming security and didn't see any issues. I had picked up on a brand-new Chevy Suburban that was on the request list. As I was making an entry, two police officers popped out of an unmarked car. I jumped from the car and the foot pursuit was on.

The getaway vehicle I was in got away, but without me. I fought off the officers as long as I could. Have you seen a movie when the people are lost at sea and could see a ship in the distance? That's how I felt, as I saw the getaway — getaway in the distance. I was finally tackled and brought down rather roughly and taken into a holding tank for booking.

After a few days, I was released on my own recognizance and went to court. I later pleaded no contest and served thirty days with restitution fines in the thousands. It was just another one of several bad decisions I made before realizing *I was doing it wrong all along.*

I was still going to school at the CDC and Judge Jones still didn't give up on me. I thought I should complete high school.

Later one day in that year of 1995, both my parents walked into the living room at our place in the projects and stood directly in front of me with their arms crossed. The stress showed heavily on their faces. It was clear that my mother had been crying. My dad pointed at me.

"Abidan, we are tired of cops breaking down our door looking for you, or stolen cars in the parking lot. We are always worrying about one of you getting shot and killed, falling into drug addiction, or going to jail for life. We are moving to Moreno Valley. Whether *you* like it or not, *we are done.*"

The following week they moved out of the projects. I stayed behind and so did my two elder brothers. I didn't want to move out. It was the life I knew and was accustomed to. I wasn't ready to change that for anything.

With my parents gone it wasn't long before we had the entire projects at our doorsteps. There was a lot of partying and fighting. My brothers and I finally moved out of the projects about one month later.

My older brothers moved in with their girlfriends, and for a few months I was moving from house to house, while trying to graduate high school. Alma? Well, she was waiting to see what my next move was going to be.

Later that summer I graduated from CDC. Judge Jones was on stage at the ceremony, and I could see his smile as I crossed the podium. I stopped for a minute to thank him.

"Judge, I just want to tell you how much I appreciate your belief in me, through some bad situations." We shook hands.

"Abidan, a lot of people have noticed your drive, as misguided as it has been from time to time. You *have* been a handful. But there is something about you that makes me think you are *driven* to find great success, and whatever it is you are after." We were still shaking hands and laughed as we released our grips.

He surprised me by pointing to my shoes.

"Hey, Abidan. Those are Stacey Adams shoes, right?"

I pulled my pant legs up slightly to show off the shoes.

"Yep." I was proud of the shoes and it showed. *Strange that the Judge noticed them.*

"Well, it may surprise you to know that I have the same pair under this robe. Look."

He pulled up the front edge of his robe. There they were.

"That's cool, Judge," I said.

"Well," the Judge replied smiling. "Remember, everyone likes quality."

Abidan and Judge Jones Chuckled about wearing the same "Stacy Adams" shoes on Graduation Day.

After graduation, I spoke to Alma. I asked her how she would feel if I moved to Moreno Valley. She was all for it but we both knew it would be a difficult relationship because she had one more year to go before graduation. We both tried. I stuck it out as long as I could but without dependable transportation it was a struggle to visit her. I had already sold the Caprice to help my parents pay the mortgage.

Moreno Valley's cost of living was far greater than living in the projects and my father started to realize that quickly. He would always walk out in the morning without knowing anyone. He found a gardening job which led to a construction job later that year.

Slowly, steadily.

Chapter 7

Marriage

Love before success can be a recipe for disaster.

Everything was different living in Moreno Valley. After a few months I was still trying to figure out how to adjust to this new and completely different city. My younger brother and I would walk the city mall to get used to this new city, but it felt odd because there was such a small population of people. On a busy Saturday morning, you would see twenty people max. We just weren't used to such a quiet place.

We met a few guys in town who started showing us around, and I slowly stopped going back to L.A. every weekend. I found a job at "Cal Spas" in Chino, but that job only lasted about two months before I quit. It wasn't for me. I just couldn't see myself painting spas for the rest of my life, especially on an assembly line with everyone around me bickering at each other.

I saved enough money to buy a new car, a 1987 Regal. I was missing my girlfriend, so I drove back to L.A. to see her. Even though our relationship didn't seem as strong as it was a year earlier, I was missing her more than ever. She visited me a few times, one of those times was New Years of 1995. She spent that New Year's Eve with me in Moreno Valley, and I drove her home back to L.A. later that night.

In January of 1996, it happened. I started working with my father in the Construction Industry. He had acquired a job at Guy Yocom Construction and they were paying him a fairly decent wage. I thought I could start working with him and maybe learn to be good at *something*. However, with no experience, the only place I was going to start was as a shovel man or "labor man".

Abidan in 1997 at the Manhattan Beach Construction Studios.

I asked my father several questions about handling a shovel, a stripping bar, a scrapper, and other miscellaneous tools. He assisted me in learning how to operate all the personal tools, but as always I wanted to learn more. I wanted to become a *Great Carpenter*, but I knew I had to demonstrate the ability to grow and become the number one laborer first. I continued as a laborer for the next several months, while Alma was on her way to graduating high school that spring of 1996.

One Saturday I asked her to go out with me for the evening. I picked her up and after a long night of having a great time, we realized the feelings between us were deep and permanent. It wasn't impulsive, or misguided by passion. It was time.

We were married June 8, 1996, and we held our reception at my older brother's house in L.A. We were cheered and congratulated by all the family. It felt good. *I married the girl of my dreams.*

Alma and Abidan tie the knot in the summer of 1996.

But overriding the joy I was feeling were the facts: I was only a laborer making $5 an hour while living in my parent's house in Moreno Valley. I was bringing home $135 a week just enough to pay rent, bills, fuel, and buy a pizza.

I knew something had to change and it had to be soon. So, one day, while my wife was at home waiting for me, I decided to go back to L.A. after work and pick up a pound of weed. I thought if I could break it up and sell it in ounces, I would make a great profit and hopefully get us a good jump start. *It was the worst decision I had ever made for us both.*

I managed to pick up the pound of marijuana. However, in the middle of the 110 freeway in South Central L.A., I was pulled over by a task force of the County Sheriffs who were doing a gang sting on all local gangs at that very moment. It made sense. Why not? Right? And there I was.

I pulled into a muffler shop and got out of the car. I was immediately arrested for possession of drugs.

My life was ruined, I thought to myself. I was just married, getting ready to start this new life. Alma was at my parents' home, and I knew *her* parents were not going to be happy about this. *What have I done?* A lot of people were going to be disappointed with me. I kept thinking for hours, and I could just envision Alma's disappointment.

When I finally got the chance to use the phone at the police station I just stood there, staring at the phone for a few minutes. I was to nervous to call, but I finally found the courage to do so.

My mother answered my call and had a lot of questions.

"What happened to you?"

I briefly spoke to her, but I wanted to speak to Alma, so my mother handed the phone over to her.

Alma knew something bad had happened, women sense those things. I explained, in short emotion-filled words, what had happened and what I had done.

"Honey, I am so sorry." I apologized profusely and promised this would never happen again. Still, a cold silence from her end of the phone. *Oh, my God, help me.*

I prayed she would understand, and I would make immediate life corrections.

She very calmly asked, "Why would you do this? Money isn't everything in this world. We had each other. And now I'm alone with your parents." I could feel the pain in her voice. It hurt. It hurt us both.

I promised her I would be out soon, and I would call her the minute I went to court for arraignment, but to my surprise, they had records of the GTA's in the projects; well, now all of the cases were against *me*. The Judge asked me what I knew about those stolen cars, and I responded that I didn't know anything.

He offered me a deal and noted that it had been over a couple of years since the events. So, if I took a deal now, I would serve one year county time and the GTA's would be dismissed. Otherwise, I would have to go to trial.

I thought I would get out in just a few weeks, but now I *was screwed*. I called Alma during the courts' recess to inform her that I would not be getting out soon. She started crying in disbelief. My poor choices had caught up to me and now it was affecting my wife and life even more.

Later that summer, Alma would move back in with her parents while I completed my time in the county jail.

A big step back.

Chapter 8

Daughter

The sound of her voice as she enters into this world.

Unbelievable! Due to overpopulated jails I was unexpectedly released a few months later, on an early release program. I was excited to get out and get back to Alma and family.

By the time I was released in late September of 1996, my wife had moved back in with her parents. They were under the impression that she was moving back in so she could return to the previous job she held prior to getting married. She never told them I was in jail, she only told them that I was working out of state and would be back soon.

I was released and ready to rebuild my life. I had done a lot of thinking while I was in Supermax, near Magic Mountain. I started reading books and planning for a better future, just as I had done once before when I was in Los Padrinos Juvenile Hall. But this time I was serious. I wanted to make immediate changes. Things were about to get interesting.

Alma had already settled back in at her parent's house in Los Angeles and had just resolved some of the differences she had with her father, and because of my last demonstrated debacle she did not want to run the risk of moving back with me to Moreno Valley. I had to make some decisions. I would either move back in with my parents alone and have a long-distance relationship once again or move in with Alma at her parent's house. We both decided I would move in with her and see how it would all play out.

A few months later after some of the chill of my mistakes warmed a bit. Alma and I went to the doctor after she started feeling nauseous. She was in the doctor's office for quite a while. Then the door swung open and she ran prancing out and jumped into my arms with a beautiful smile wrapped around her beaming face.

"What!? What? Honey, *what?*"

"I'm pregnant!" Tears were flooding her eyes.

It was an overjoying feeling that only living through that moment could explain. Unreal, and yet such a beautiful moment.

For the next several months we both would work and save money for our newborn to come in the summer of '97. While still living with my in-laws, I continued to work construction jobs, even though the pay was the same as before I got arrested, which was $5.00 an hour.

We returned to the doctor to find out the gender and were excited to learn it was going to be a girl. We both started writing possible names for the next few months until the birth of our new baby.

On a Thursday night, Alma's water broke and I rushed her to the doctor. Later the next night, I witnessed the birth and crying voice of my beautiful daughter. I cradled our new baby in my arms for the first time while sitting close to Alma in her hospital bed. We both stared at her with a wonderful almost indefinable feeling of love flowing over us. *We* had made this beautiful baby together. Stephanie Jasmin Padilla was born on July 11, 1997.

Our families both came together permanently to celebrate the birth of our daughter. For years to come that great relationship between both families remains unified.

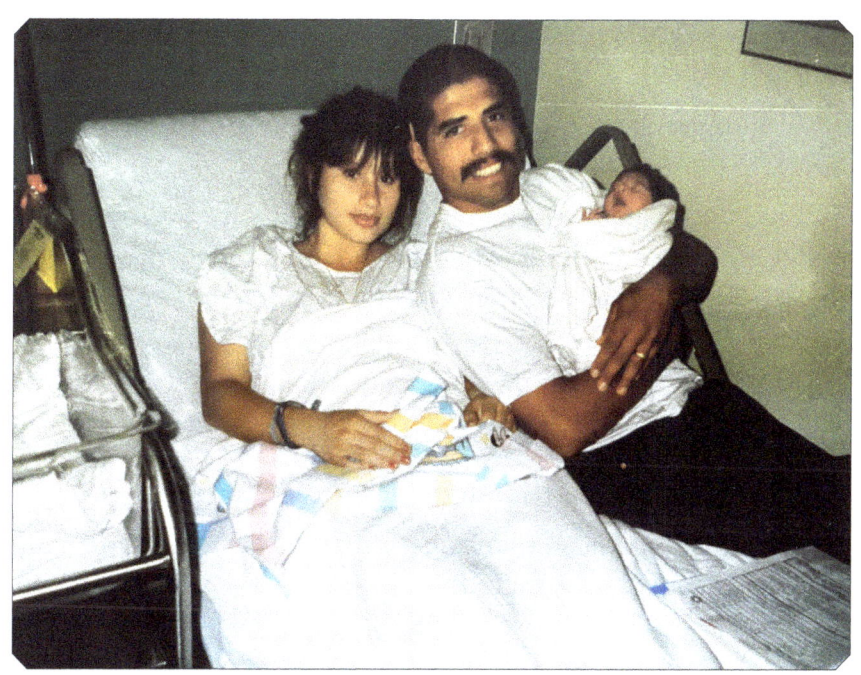

Welcoming our first-born Stephanie J. Padilla into our lives on this special day, July 11, 1997.

A few months after my daughter's birth I moved back into my parent's house in Moreno Valley because I wasn't at all interested in living in L.A. any longer. After all, *I was now a parent* and was ready for change.

Alma was also ready. However, she made it clear that she would only move in with me if we had our own place. After about a month of living with my parents, I asked my mother if she could help me with her credit score so we could get our place. She did. Soon after, my wife, daughter, and I moved into our very first apartment in Riverside, California, close to Morena Valley.

* * * * *

I continued to work hard to get a raise, however labor work was not cutting it for me. I knew if I wanted to move up, I would have to approach things differently. I had an idea.

One day, while at work, I spoke to Matt in the office. He was one of the foremen.

"Hey, Matt." I pointed at the stack of blueprints on the drafting table.

"I wonder if there is an old set of blueprints that I might have."

He looked at me strangely and looked into my eyes as if searching for something. Then he moved over to the stack of prints and after a brief search, pulled a large roll out and handed it to me.

"What are you planning to do with them?"

"I'm going to learn how to read them."

He smiled and said, "Best of luck." as he walked away.

I would read those plans every day after work until 2 a.m. for the next two years, including the weekends. *I was hungry for success! I wanted to know everything.*

In the meantime, while on the job I continued working my way up the ladder by learning different means and methods.

On a Friday after work, I went to cash my check so I could pay the rent. After the rent was paid, we only had about $10 for that entire weekend. We bought our daughter food and a $5 pizza that would last as our dinner for the week. Alma was by my side completely and understood that things were going to get better. Her support and love strengthened my resolve.

After asking for a couple of raises throughout 1997, I managed to get up to about $9.50 an hour. We were still just getting by. Alma was a genuine homemaker, taking care of our growing daughter. And me? I was *dedicated* to continuing the search for success in the construction industry.

Finally, I got the opportunity to demonstrate to everyone what I had learned, and I was confident I could handle it after studying the blueprints for endless hours. I was dug in. I *wanted* to show what I could do.

A Foreman by the name of Angelo Romeo gave me that chance. I started to layout footings and building panels, and although I made some minor mistakes, he could see I was on the right track. That went on for several months. I had never been afraid to ask for raises and I did so again but was brusquely told "NO" by the General Superintendent. He also stated that it would be a long time before I would receive another raise.

I didn't understand. I was doing the work of a lead man but only getting paid as a laborer. I was later told by the Foreman that I would have to wait a few years before I could make $20 an hour, maybe even 10 years. That's what *he* said.

I was in disbelief and would not accept that. I refused to allow someone else to direct my future and for some undefined reason want to keep me from *moving on up*. (Like the TV show, "The Jefferson's").

Chapter 9

Taste of Success

The moment your financial life shows you that hard work counts.

I continued on my defined road to success, and *nothing* was going to stop me now. I kept reading the blueprints and asking questions. Sometimes my questions would get repetitive, but I would still ask daily, and that's how I gained my knowledge.

One Thursday morning, while at work at one of our jobs in Manhattan Beach, the company gave me a van with a gas card so I could drive my crew from Riverside into the L.A. area. This was an apparent attempt to discourage me from asking for another raise.

Little did they know I was *not* going to quit trying. A group of us were on the way to a jobsite one morning and I was talking with one of the employees in the van.

"Why don't you run work as a Foreman?" he said. "You can do it, and if not here, you can go somewhere else."

I thought about it for a week or so and discussed it with my wife over a cold pizza and the half gallon of milk we had left in our fridge. My wife was on my side as she has always been all along. Together we decided to go for it.

The following week I built up enough courage to make the first major decision in what was going to be one of several to follow. I informed my father that I would not be going to work that Friday and asked if he could drive the company van to work along with all the employees, and he agreed.

I then drove onto a new job site in Temecula, California, The name of the project: "Temecula Business Park".

I spoke to a guy by the name of Ray Herbs. He was brusque.

"What do you want?"

I was somewhat nervous but confident in my approach, I said, "I'm looking for a carpenter's position."

He asked, "are you a carpenter?"

I replied, "yes."

He looked me over briefly then said, "put your bags on and get to work!"

I ran to my car to get my bags and realized I had left them inside the van that morning,

Oh, No. What am I going to do? I asked myself.

I walked back towards Foreman Ray and told him I forgot my tool bags. He was surprised. He rolled his eyes and pursed his lips.

"Okay, then. Get a shovel and start working."

Several thoughts ran through my mind. *Not the shovel again.* I visualized myself shoveling concrete for endless hours. Suddenly I had a thought.

I said to him, "If you will let me work tomorrow, I will work for *free* and if you like my work, we can discuss my rate at the end of the day."

He seemed a bit jolted by what I said.

"Let's see." He tilted his face down slightly and looked at me with a slight smile. "You'll work a whole day for free if I don't like your work?"

I put my hands on my hips and stood directly in front of him.

"Yes. That's right. I will."

He agreed to give me a shot. It was going to be free if he didn't like my work anyway, so I guess he figured *why not*?

The following day was a Saturday. I showed up ready to go in at 5 a.m. sharp. I had my bags in hand this time and a couple of year's worth of blueprints that I had read in my apartment kitchen. *This is my secret weapon, and this would be my chance.* I told myself as soon as I get an opportunity, I will show him I know how to read the plans.

I started off building panel forms and slab header. And everything was moving along great. A guy by the name of Luke came over and asked if I could help him set up a few embeds in the foundation, and I agreed to help him. I recall immediately seeing that Luke was setting the embed facing the wrong direction.

"Luke," I said. "Take a look at how you've set this embed. See anything wrong with it?"

He bent over the settings and studied them for a while.

"Well, I don't see any – " He suddenly leaned forward and fixed his eyes on the settings. "Oh my gosh. I think they're set wrong."

He then called Ray over.

"Hey, Ray. Take a look at these settings. Did I set them in the right direction?"

Ray bent over and looked at the settings. It didn't take him long. He was matter-of-fact.

"Wrong direction. Do it over."

He paused and faced Luke.

"Good thing you caught it. It would have bad, and expensive to tear it out and repair."

"Ray," Luke said. "Abidan found it."

During lunchtime I sat by myself. I noticed a few guys talking to Ray by his truck and wondered what they were discussing. Someone finally said, "Okay. Roll it up. It's time to call it a day."

I started to pick up tools and Ray walked over to me.

"How much do you want an hour?"

I wasn't sure, because I never made more than $9.50 an hour.

After waiting on me for a minute or two he answered his own question.

"How about $19 an hour?" Ray suggested.

I think my response was automatic. I had already learned, *being challenged all my childhood*, that there is something inside me which drives me about the mysterious need of making instant responses.

Now that he initiated the starting wage I said, "How about $20?" As if I wanted to negotiate.

Then he said, "No. That won't work. How about $19?"

After about 20 seconds I said, "You got a deal. Thanks, Ray."

We shook hands.

I had thought I'd try to play hardball for a few seconds, but I didn't want to risk my *100% pay increase!* So it was done. I was super excited. I immediately called Alma, dad, and everyone I could. My life was finally about to change.

A few days after I started working with Ray, I asked him if I could bring on my father who was also a great carpenter.

He smiled and said, "Sure. Bring him on."

To this day, my father still works with me.

My first paycheck at Spur Concrete Inc. was unreal, like something out of the movies. I showed it to Alma with a flair of dramatics in the presentation. She screamed with laughter and joy, and we danced around the living room. We could finally afford more than just pizza for dinner on the weekends.

Now I wanted to move out of the apartment and buy our own home in Moreno Valley. I approached Alma about it. Cautiously.

"No." She was adamant. "I'm *not* going to follow you as I did when we were living at my parent's house."

However, I wasn't taking "no" for an answer again, and this time I had my mind made up. And my way. We bought our first home in the late summer of 1998 in Moreno Valley. I was 21 years old.

First Home - Gets a new basketball court.

After moving into our first home, I would continue to elevate my construction knowledge. Alma acquired a full-time job as a QC employee for a warehouse in Riverside. My young daughter Stephanie would go to my mother's house daily, for she would be her babysitter for the next few years.

I would go on to sell the house a few years later and make a great profit. Then I went on to buy another home. We would continue that process for the next several years.

* * * * *

I would move on to follow Ray Herbs to the next company Kendrick Construction Services, as his lead man, and by this time the pay raises came more frequently.

One afternoon I was approached by Steve Fisher. He was the General Superintendent at the time and was well-known in the construction tilt-up community. We sat down in his office and he peered over his glasses at me across his desk.

"How old are you? How do you know so much at this young age?"

I was enthusiastic but forced myself to be calm.

"I'm 22. It's just been all the hard work I put in when no one else is watching, extra hours of studying, lots of reading and asking questions!"

He then looked me directly in the eye.

"Do you want to be a Foreman?"

I was caught by surprise but answered honestly.

"I don't have the skills required to schedule, coordinate, or run work."

Steve's response bounced my mind.

"You either want to be bossed or want to be the boss, you choose."

The next Monday I was on my first four-building project as a Foreman, at the age of 22 years old. Steve came by that morning to give a quick intro into the life of a foreman and I was on my own. I think he knew what he found; a "Diamond in the Rough." I was excited to share the news with everyone around me. It was a dream come true.

After a few years of working with Steve, I felt it was time for me to make my next move, once again, seeking a better opportunity.

Steve was in the mix of starting his own company and I made sure to reassure him that I would consider coming back once he got his company going.

We were both on good terms.

A good thing.

Chapter 10

Son

*The smile on his face
and the strength he brings into this world.*

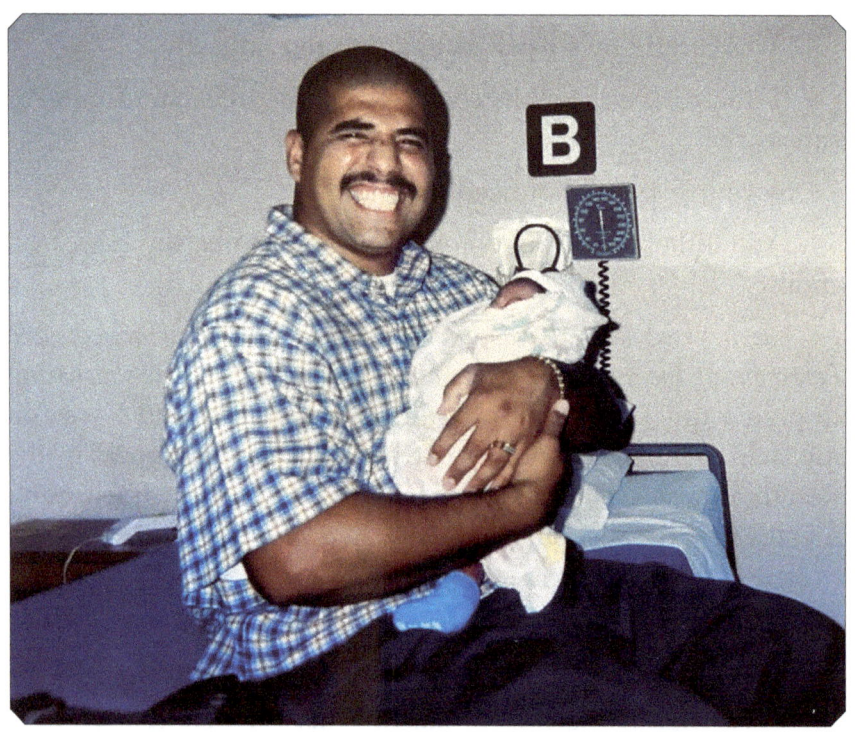

*Abidan super excited with the birth of his son Austin Padilla,
on this special day of July 29, 2002.*

Abidan Austin Padilla, Jr. arrived in the summer of 2002. Alma and I celebrated the birth of our new baby boy with great excitement. He was born on July 29, 2002, with a wonderful smile on his face. Austin would bring floods of happiness to our family. And now his sister would have a baby boy whom she could love and help in his care.

Alma stopped working, and I continued my rigorous/vigorous approach with an even more enhanced appetite to learn everything I possibly could. I went on to work for RC Construction Services on school projects dealing with DSA inspectors. I wanted to "master" this trade from all angles: CIP walls, Slabs, Foundations, and Tilt-ups on both public and private projects.

The following year Alma went out home shopping in a newly-built community near the Moreno Valley Mall. Later that evening we talked.

"Well," I ventured cautiously, remembering our last encounter on this subject, "how did it go?"

"Abidan." There was a coy smile teasing the corner of her mouth.

Hmm. I wonder what this is all about.

"Abidan," she said again, lowering her chin and looking out over the top of her big eyes, almost seductively. *"You are going to have to go out and see the model homes that are being built."*

"Why? Are the builders doing something wrong?"

"No, there's nothing wrong." She took a deep breath and gave me a big smile. "Abidan, I *like* them!"

I was astounded.

The next day we went to go look at the homes together, and to my continued surprise, we both found them unique, appealing, and quality-built. After a fun-filled search, we found one that we both agreed upon.

We sold out first home almost immediately, made a great profit, and moved into our new home. Austin was almost one year old, and Stephanie was five. We were excited and proud.

Over the next few years, we designed our exterior yard to our tastes and hosted several family events. We celebrated Austin's second birthday and even rented a small train that took all the kids around the block. The kids loved it, laughing and shouting. There were also lots of games and a few piñatas.

On weekends we would walk our kids to the nearby park and play basketball on the small court at home. Austin was growing up fast and becoming an athlete. He would make long shots as if he was a natural. Stephanie was a big cute girl now and doing cheerleading and attending city parades.

I was now twenty-seven years of age, raising a beautiful family, and somehow would find time to go out and have a few drinks back at my older brother's home in L.A., *without* Alma's consent. — *Oops*. She caught me on my cell. I could feel the heat.

"I suppose you're at your brother's place in L.A.?"

Uh, oh. She wanted *no* part of our former lives in L.A.

"Well," I said carefully, "things are different here now, and I thought - "

"You *thought?*" She was ticked. "Why didn't you *think* to talk to me about it?"

Alma was strong. I couldn't come up with anything to say. I was suddenly feeling guilty.

Silence from both ends.

"Alma," I said, but realized she had hung up.

My older brother, Epi ,was the only one that decided to stay back and didn't want to move. My second older brother, Chago, was now down five years of his eight-year sentence.

So my younger brother Jose and I were the only ones from my family working alongside my father on construction projects.

*****

After a couple of years working as a foreman for RC Construction, I received a phone call from Saul Garcia, who was the Union BA the time. He was a great man who seemed to genuinely care for the employees he represented.

Saul was calling to inform me that Steve wanted to speak with me and wanted to know if I could call him back. I was hesitant to respond to Saul because I wasn't ready to leave RC after only just two years. It was awkward. I didn't call Steve.

A couple of weeks went by and I received a call from my father who was working at a different location.

"Hey, Son. How are you?"

"I'm doing great, Dad. Just busy. Very busy."

"Listen. Saul Garcia stopped by the worksite, and wanted to know why you didn't call Steve."

"Dad, I've only been with RC two years. And I have a good relationship there. I'm reluctant to leave so early."

"I'm surprised. It's not your style to not look at an open door. You've always pounced on opportunities. And you don't even know what this is all about."

I was silent for about twenty seconds or so.

"Are you still there?" my dad finally asked. "Look, you don't have to commit, just listen to what he has to say."

I sighed. "Okay, Dad. I'll give him a call. Say hello to the rest of the crew for me."

It was late in the day, and I watched as the horizon started to show shades of bright orange. I breathed in the freshness of the fading day.

After a few days, I called Steve. He was hard to read and I wasn't sure if he was happy to hear from me. But he wasn't sad. To the contrary.

"Abidan." I could hear and feel the excitement in his voice. He jumped right into it. "My Division 3 Concrete company is now in full operating mode!"

"Wow, Steve! That's great" I couldn't help it. Steve's excitement was infectious. "Tell me about it."

"I was surprised at the reaction regarding potential work." He took a breath. "I *have* to make a move for new personnel soon. There is a lot of quality work to be had. Right now."

I could hear some hesitancy in his voice as he paused for a moment.

"Abidan. I *need* your expertise. Would you please come and join me? I'll make it worth your while."

"Hey, guy. That's a huge compliment. Thanks! Steve, can I think about it over the holidays? That should give me time to consider it."

"Yep. Of course. I can wait and will be here. Busy. Abidan, don't wait too long."

I continued to think about the new opportunity for the next few months. December of 2003 came around and we decided to host Christmas at our house. Alma and I invited both sides of our families to join us that year.

I remember going upstairs to take an overhead picture of the families. It was a Christmas that I would forever hold close to my heart. The photos froze those moments. Such beautiful times with all of our family.

We would need them.

Chapter 11

Family Loss

An unexpected heartfelt pain that would last forever.

I was planning to contact Steve and schedule a meeting after New Years. However, Our lives were changed forever with an unexpected devastating event.

At 4 a.m. on an overcast Monday morning, January 2004, my sister-in-law, Vivian, called. She was crying hysterically over the phone and I couldn't do anything but listen.

"Abidan," she sobbed. "Something terrible has happened." She broke down again. Her words were incomprehensible.

"Vivian, try to calm down." I feared terrible news because of Vivian's condition. My heart tightened. "What is it? What happened?"

"Abidan."

She broke into deep crying again. She finally blurted it out.

"I think your brother has died."

I immediately dropped to my knees and started to pray, and cry, asking myself, *"why, why God, why?"* I couldn't contain myself. Alma was trying to console me, and something inside of me exploded. My kids woke up to a screaming roar of rage coming from their daddy, and both started to cry. Alma gathered them into her arms and they all cried deeply.

I went inside the bathroom where I stayed until I was able to gather my thoughts and at least some control of my grief and anger. After several minutes and lots of deep breaths, I called my father to inform him of what just occurred. He was the strongest of both my parents and I knew I couldn't tell my mother her son just died.

"Dad," I said in a voice I barely recognized, "I don't know what happened, but I'm going to drive there immediately and find out."

"Son," he said in a subdued but surprisingly calm voice. "Don't go. I want to find out what happened before we decide what to do."

At around 7 a.m. Alma and I and the kids drove to my father's house. We found my mother on the couch, in a fetal position, crying deeply and crushed in the worst mental pain and sadness of her entire life. Alma rushed to her side began to hug her closely, trying desperately to console her.

We learned that they too had spoken to Vivian. She confirmed my brother had been shot multiple times and died arriving at General Hospital in Los Angeles.

* * * * *

Just a few weeks earlier my brother and I were having a casual conversation.

"Abidan," he smiled softly. "Could you do me the favor of making sure I have shoes on when I die?"

I asked why, and he replied, "I don't want to leave this place barefooted."

"Okay, Bro. I will."

I didn't get it, but I made sure I kept my promise.

When he was taken to the mortuary, I went to visit one day before the day of the viewing. I had the pair of shoes he had asked for. I opened the casket and put them on him, and I then sat down next to him and conjured up all our childhood memories while tears were running down the side of my face.

I called the Indiana Prison warden and asked to speak to my second older brother who was only a couple of years away from being released.

When my brother finally came to the phone, I was holding the phone to my ear while staring at my entire family in front of me who appeared to be in a state of shock. Everyone was silent for a few seconds while my brother kept asking "hello, hello," several times.

I finally came to my senses and responded.

"Hello, brother. I have some bad news."

I had to take a moment. The phone line stayed silent for a while.

"What happened, Abidan?" I could hear the fear in his voice.

"We lost our brother, Epi."

As strong a person he was, I could hear him catching his breath and breathing heavily. After a few minutes, I explained to him briefly what I was told by Vivian. He paused and was quiet.

"Abidan, take care of yourself and our family."

He assured us that he would be home soon.

I could imagine the pain and desperation he went through while being locked up, but I felt the responsibility of sharing the news with him. No matter the circumstance, I knew no time was a good time to inform him his brother had died. I didn't speak to him again until he was released in 2006.

It took several months for me to mourn for my brother before I finally went back to work. I still see the pain in my parent's eyes when we talk about him. My brother had three beautiful kids who are now young adults. I'm proud of their accomplishments. I have no doubt in my mind that Epi was there watching them grow all along.

I didn't return to work for the next several weeks. Later that month I resigned from RC Construction, uncertain of the financial impact it would have on us. My wife and I were determined to be there as long as we could for Vivian and the kids, as a support system. They now moved near our home and we developed spending more time together.

I was finally ready to get back to work, so I called Steve one afternoon to schedule a meeting to discuss my return to

Division 3 Concrete. We negotiated the wages, bonus package, and off I went. I got back into the groove of things and dove right into nine tilt-up buildings in Upland, California.

A few weeks later, I brought my father back to work with me. He needed to get back to work just as I did. Believe me, working together helped strengthen our families. We were there to be the shoulders to cry on when we got home, to show encouragement in the time of vulnerability, and to simply find a way through all of this, even though it felt as if there was no way.

We gather together every year on my brother's birthday, and we celebrate his life and his beautiful memories here on earth. His warm heart and kindness will forever be remembered by everyone who knew him.

Growing up he would say to me: "Follow your dreams, I want you to be the difference. You are smart and very intelligent."

And for that brother, *thank you!*

Visiting my brother's grave at Rose Hills Cemetery.
"In Loving Memory of Epi"

Chapter 12

Personal Goals

*To understand where you're going in life
is to understand who you really are.*

I continued to work with Division 3 Concrete, raising several millions worth of square feet of buildings throughout Southern California. I had a plan. However, I had not written down all my goals in chronological order. Despite my strong drives, I was *scatterbrained*, so to speak.

In the spring of 2005, my wife and I thought it would be a great idea to move once again and so we sold our home. We would get the biggest payday at that time, we were able to make over $200K on the sale. We also had purchased five acres along with my younger brother, in Cabazon. However, we hadn't sold the acres yet. We were still waiting for the right time.

We bought a 3,300 square foot home, and we vowed it would be the last home we would purchase. We lived in that home for over 13 years, with a 20% down payment on a $500K home in 2006. We felt good about the purchase, but didn't understand the (ARM) loan well enough to know something wasn't right.

I was also working on my contractor's license and would achieve the acquisition of the CSLB C-8 License in 2006. Once I acquired my C-8 License, I spoke to Steve and informed him that I would be making a solo attempt at running my own business now that I had my license. He told me to give it some time to think it over closely. He thought we could work something out. I was determined to start my own business, but I still wanted to hear what he had to say.

A couple of days went by, Steve and I finally talked, and worked something out. Steve offered to promote me up to an

RME/General Superintendent. Shortly after I would complete the greatest accomplishment of my construction career, which was the building of the magnificent "Bass Pro Shops" in Rancho Cucamonga, CA.

The project consisted of multiple concrete elements such as Tilt-Up Walls, CIP Walls, CMU Wall, Steel Decks, and a massive Foundation with an unbelievable Architectural Finished Floor. I took personal joy in building the aquariums with a stream with fish swimming it, and the Hunting Department with bear claw trails leading up to it.

The ground-breaking at the incredible Bass Pro Shops in 2006 went well. It was a spectacular building, and quickly became one of the most popular visitor sites in the area.

My last Foreman project before becoming General Superintendent.

For the next few years, I was the General Superintendent overseeing the entire company. With over ten Foreman, three hundred employees, and over fifteen projects ranging from Two Million to Ten Million dollars each, we were one of the biggest companies in concrete at that time.

* * * * *

After moving into our new home, I started writing down my goals in 2007, and I would read them daily. I wanted to achieve great heights, provide a good life for my family, and pay my kids' college tuitions.

I would continue to improve my computer skills and my vocabulary skills by reading lots of books. I would also create word documents to assist our daily work schedules, which several General Contractors found helpful, and contributed suggestions to help improve the template.

I asked a lot of questions and listened more than anything, in my drive to not miss out on any words of wisdom. I immensely enjoyed reading the book by Anthony Robbins called *Unlimited Power*. In his book, Robbins says the following, "If you want to achieve success, all you need to do is find a way to model those who have already succeeded."

Now, it doesn't sound difficult to do, *but have you started yet?* The biggest challenge can be you. *Yes, you. If you don't start, you'll never know what it could have been.*

I went on to read several books and every single book I read was great. You just have to get started. *The beginning is always the hardest, but it will all come together.*

One afternoon I went to my first negotiation meeting with Steve and the Subs. Steve had over $100K in back charges on this particular project due to job conditions and other delays that were being pinned on us. I gathered information and put together a timeline of emails and additionally signed backups to cross-reference at the meeting. It was a good thing I was able to do that because we were able to walk out of that meeting with a zero balance.

My pay raises and bonuses were looking a lot better after that meeting. It's all part of the preparation: You may have all the information, but I strongly believe it's how you present it. *Reading books has sure paid off,* I thought.

Later that year, we flew out to South Dakota for pheasant hunting. It was a great experience with upper-echelon business owners, and I started to understand the meaning of "work hard and play hard."

After one week in South Dakota, it was back to work. We started multiple buildings in San Diego, where I trained a few other lead men into the foreman position. We were expanding rapidly, and I was excited about the future of Division 3. My Goals were lining up with what was going on at that time, and I was bringing people up with me to train into better positions. It was a win-win for everyone.

With more to come.

Chapter 13

Coaching Sports

If it doesn't challenge you, it doesn't change you.

Alma and I decided it was time to get our kids into sports. Stephanie was now nine years old and Austin was four. We went to the local recreation park and signed Austin up for T-ball and Stephanie would follow the next season with softball.

I remember recording every game Austin played in, and later met the coach who would then ask me to help with the fields. I volunteered periodically and learned how to socialize with other people; something that I wasn't used to coming from a community that had the mindset of "to each his own."

When I returned home from work I would check the game schedule calendar, and then get so excited that I would take my kids out to practice before a game. I never played baseball, however, I remember walking my younger brother to his baseball games on 108th St. when we were about 10 years old.

One Saturday afternoon I was playing catch with Austin while Stephanie was having softball practice with her team called the "Wildfire", when the team mom walked up to my wife and asked her if I would like to help coach. Without checking with me first Alma's response was "yes." Later that evening when she informed me that I was a coach. I didn't know how to react then I looked at Stephanie and she smiled, that's all that was said.

I bought a few baseball and softball books and taught myself how to become a good coach. For the next several months we would help both Austin's and Steph's teams. I coached and Alma volunteered at the fundraisers.

The next summer, in 2009, I made a run for head coach of

Stephanie's softball team called the "Roadrunners." Our team had a rough season, but lots of good friendships were made originating from a guy that had once been bad at socializing with other people.

I have to say I owe it all to Alma. After that season was all over I was encouraged by several of the parents to continue coaching. Apparently, everyone thought we did just fine and so I continued to coach for several more seasons.

The next spring season the competitive edge was at its highest, and I sincerely wanted to win, but we came in 2nd place. I went back to coach that fall season at the recreational park at a final attempt to winning the 1st place championship trophy and it was all worth it, my daughter Stephanie pitched a great game that night.

All the team players and parents were happy "we did it," 1st Place Champions… the next move for the entire team was competitive Travel Softball.

I would also help assist coach my son Austin's travel baseball team. The fall of 2010 "SoCal Knuckle Up 14U Padilla" was established. The team would go on to play together until they were an 18U team and most of the players got recruited to play in college. Both my wife and I found a new passion for teaching and a competitive itch for winning.

The 16U Padilla team was fun to watch. The defensive synchronization was unreal. If you were in the stands you would stand the chance of falling out of your seats as you watched this team play. A few triple plays would get us an opportunity to win a championship title at a Triple Crown event. We did have some losses, but not against other 16U teams, we would always play up with the 18U teams.

Several months later, we traveled to San Diego for the Showcase by the Sea, Triple Crown Tournament. On Saturday Knuckle Up 16U Padilla would play 3 pool games, which we won. The following day we would be 1st seed in our bracket and would eliminate every team we faced that day.

The Local San Diego Team., "Power Surge," would do the same in their bracket and met us later that night for the championship game. The opposing team took an early lead and would score a run per inning. We were cold and couldn't get a run across after sitting out for several hours waiting for this game.

We were the home team and down 7-0, so I huddled the entire team together at the bottom of the 7th inning and said to everyone, "No matter what happens here we have already won, now let's go out there and take it a pitch at a time and find a way to get on base. Let's play for fun now."

The pressure was off and the team looked reenergized. The bats come out with discipline swinging at good pitches only. Before we knew it, we were tied 7-7 with 2 outs and bases loaded, one run away from another championship title. What a game it was. People in the stands were jumping and shouting.

We would go on to lose the game in the 9th inning in a California tie-breaker. The final score was 7-8. SoCal Knuckle Up as an organization gained a lot of respect and recognition from the top teams in the softball world.

Later on we traveled to other events such as the Colorado Sparkler Tournament where we placed 3rd in the bronze bracket out of over 150 teams nationwide.

*****

Austin went on to Travel Baseball for the next few years. He is now first string high school varsity player hitting well over a .300 batting average. Austin will be majoring in Business and wants to attend the University of California at Riverside.

Stephanie is a senior in college majoring in psychology and currently working as a Teacher in the Riverside school district.

Coaching - while Stephanie is the winning run at 3rd base at a Triple Crown tournament.

Austin goes deep for a stand-up double vs Temecula Canyon High.

Chapter 14

Business Owners

Falling down only counts if you don't get back up.

Stronger Together

I continued to work at Division Three. Now as a General Superintendent I was able to make my own work schedule. Coaching sports was my number one priority and I would do anything to make it all work out just to see the smiles on my kids' faces.

I also purchased an investment home, a single-story property sitting on a half an acre with a rental trailer in the back. I kept this property and rented it for a few years while the economy grew.

Later that fall of 2009, I started to notice a decrease in the number of projects we were being awarded. The projects were all coming to an end, and our employees were starting to get laid off.

One morning I met with Steve over a cup of coffee and asked him about this.

"What do you think will happen next year in terms of a strong economy?"

His response was unclear and uncertain.

"Abidan, I just don't know. I've been watching it, but – " He shrugged his shoulders. That was enough for me. I started to prepare for the worst recession yet. It was projected to take place soon.

A few weeks later I disassociated my C8 License from Division Three Concrete, and shortly after I called Steve to inform him that I was going to be moving on to pursue other endeavors. He was shocked that I would be making this move with a very uncertain economy blanketing us.

I decided it was now or never. Soon enough AP Concrete Construction was born. I completely dived in and landed a few projects that kept several employees busy. These guys had been working with me for several years at Division Three and now they were ready to be a part of AP Concrete.

AP Concrete was not a big company. However, we were kept very busy through the first couple of years of the recession. Alma and I would handle all the office admin work, all the estimating, and sometimes I would also work out in the field.

After a couple of years, a few general contractors started to hold on to the retention, so I was forced to put the company on hold while I figured out what to do next. I would be on unemployment for the very first time in my life.

My home was now going into the modification program

that would last two years before it finally got worked out.

I applied to several construction companies but with the resume I had, I was immediately denied each time. Everyone would tell me, "Sorry. You are overqualified."

I then went to my union business agent and received an unpleasant comment, "Abidan," he said with downcast eyes, "we can't keep everyone busy." He then recommended I call a non-union company.

I could not believe what I heard, but after several months of no job opportunities, I did just that. I contacted a non-union company manager who immediately thought of my resume as an opportunity to acquire a well-qualified employee for a very low wage. I couldn't do anything else but to accept the chance at getting back to work even if it meant taking a *60% pay cut.*

Later that day I thought to myself, *if I go work for a company while making less than carpenter wages, I would be able to have my home approved for the modification.* So that's exactly what I did. For the next two years, I would work making $16 per hour in hopes of negotiating my home.

It was now several years since I sat down in my home office and wrote down all my goals. There were no positive signs of a prosperous future on the horizon, and I was starting to lose faith. However, I didn't want to convey that to my family, so I continued to wake up daily and pray to our lord for what we did have, which was God, family, health, friends, and now once again work.

I finally received a call from the bank, and they informed me that our modification has been approved. We could not believe what they did to help us. The original loan amount was reduced by over 50%.

Alma and I prayed daily and thanked Saint Expedite, Jesus, and Mary through the almighty power of our Lord God. We were full of joy, so much stress was suddenly lifted off both of us. The following month our new payment was down significantly, and I knew I was ready to make my next financial move.

I continued to work as a carpenter and a few months later I was promoted to a foreman. Everyone in the tilt-up industry would call the owner of that company and would say to him, "Do you realize who's working for you?" He finally recognized I was not only a foreman but *a person*. But after building a couple of million-dollar projects for him, it was time to move on.

After going over a couple of years with a pay cut, I thought it was time for me to regain my position. I formulated a contract explaining in detail what I was asking for in terms of a salary package agreement. I also consulted Mr. Zavala, my good friend and attorney, for assistance in formulating the contract.

Chapter 15

Real Estate Investments

*Multiple sources of income
makes for a great financial cushion.*

You should ask yourself, *how do I get started?* Well, I remember asking myself the same question. Just like with my C8 concrete license, I educated myself in real estate investment. I attended seminars and spent countless hours reading about foreclosure, short sale, wholesale properties, and any pertinent subject.

After the modification of my own home, I was finally paid the retention for the projects that I'd completed. Both Alma and I thought it was a good idea to modify the rental property since the market was low and our credit was never affected.

The modification was approved on the investment home. We would rent it out for the next few years acquiring a monthly positive cash flow. We then contacted a good friend of ours who we met in sports, who happened to be in real estate. I requested that she give comps in the surrounding areas.

It would be a buyer's market for the next year or so. I continued patiently waiting for the right time to sell. In the summer of 2014, I thought it was time. We put the home on the market and strategically priced it about 10% higher than the comps, so our profit on this home was to be well over $100K.

The home sold for our asking price in early 2015 and we were thrilled. We immediately continued on the search for our next investment home, and luckily enough by November of 2015, we found it. We purchased this home for $225K and remodeled the most obvious areas, including the kitchen and bathrooms.

This property also was a great investment, and I rented it for a couple of years acquiring a monthly positive cash flow while juggling time working on my new contract, coaching sports with the kids, and real estate investments. I knew I was on the right track to reaching the goals I had written down several years earlier.

But I also understood I had a lot of work ahead of me. My daughter was graduating high school and moving on to college. Alma and I were extremely proud of her. Later that fall of 2015, we dropped her off at the campus dorms and as we drove away it felt significantly different. We were happy yet sad at the same time, but we knew deep down it was time for her to experience life on her own.

My son was on his way to high school that year. He continued to play travel baseball and I continued to coach him. I knew coaching was soon coming to an end for me since my daughter was now in college, and my son would soon be in high school playing high school ball.

Taking a break: Family vacation in Costa Rica

Never losing sight of my goals, I continued to move forward. Even when times were not looking too promising, I would find ways to encourage myself. Alma did the same, and she thought it was time for her to finally get back into the workforce after helping me with our construction company.

Alma applied for the MVUSD and was hired shortly thereafter. She is currently a nutrition manager at one of the largest schools in our community.

For the next few years, we would focus on our jobs and raising our kids while managing our investments.

One afternoon while coaching my son's baseball game I started talking to Eddie He was a good friend of ours and also a baseball coach.

"Hey Eddie," I asked. "What type of work do you do?"

"I am a CSLB Private Investigator."

"Really?" I was surprised. "I'm a CSLB Private Investigator too. I've been a CSLB contractor and have been for several years now."

"Well." he said matter-of-factly. "That's good. Then I suggest that you apply for a private inspector position since you've had a C* license for over five years. It's an interesting job," he added. "It consists of generating inspection reports and submitting them to CSLB Investigators once completed. Pretty simple and direct."

"Hmmm." I thought about it briefly as I glanced out at the playing field. "I don't know, Eddie. My schedule is jammed. I don't know if I could do it justice."

"Well, the fact is that the inspections would only take a few hours weekly. You should be able to handle that easily. And don't forget:" he added. *"You can make up to $500 per report."*

After hearing that, I went in and applied. It paid off. Today I have done over one hundred inspections on my schedule or weekends. It has been a great side job for me, and it continues to bring in extra cash.

* * * * *

Do you want to know your net worth? First, examine your network. Success is there for everyone, and I strongly believe *it starts with writing down and reading your personal goals daily and then taking action.* That has worked for me. It doesn't happen overnight, but in order to sleep better at night *it has to happen.*

Chapter 16

Persistence Through Recession

*It's not about how many times you've fallen,
it's about you getting back up every time.*

After several years of ongoing financial stressful days, there was finally light at the end of the tunnel. We continued on our path to reach our goals. Alma and I would go on to learn more about her daily work and would get better every day.

Both of our kids continued to achieve great academics. Each day as they were growing, they were learning more about their futures. I felt good about our current situation and continued on the search for success on multiple levels. I took what life had to offer. I was grateful every day for waking up just to have another chance to get better at life.

After going well over a couple of years with a pay cut, I thought it was time for me to regain my position. I formulated a contract explaining in detail what I was asking for in terms of a salary package agreement.

I went on to make a few copies and would pass it out to several companies who showed a high interest in interviewing me. I only made it to one interview and then suddenly, out of nowhere I received a call from K.C, the owner of KCB Builders Inc.

K.C and I had a great phone conversation and scheduled a formal meeting. I met with him on the agreed time for the interview and presented my contract. K.C was quiet while he was looking over it. After a brief moment, he asked about my successful and impressive history.

"Abidan, I would like to know more about you." He paused. "What would you guarantee me if I brought you in? I recognize your past accomplishments, *but that was then, and this is now.*"

I was confident about my ability to make KCB successful again, since they appeared to be in the same situation after the collapse of the economy.

"K.C., what is your company's current annual gross revenue?"

"Between two and five million."

I paused for a few seconds while I mentally considered how my past accomplishments might fit in.

I looked K.C. right in the eye and said to him, "Not only will we grow KCB up to a 30 million yearly company, but I'll make sure I bring aboard quality personnel that I have trained over the past several years. *And,* I will introduce you to my successful past clients who will provide us continuing opportunities for growth."

After about an hour's conversation, I left with a gut feeling that I *would* be getting a call back in the coming days. I was satisfied with the results of my interview and even mentioned to K.C that I would keep him in mind when attending another interview I had lined up.

I left the interview, then about ten minutes of driving towards my next appointment, my phone rang. It was Barbara, K.C's wife. Barbara had been sitting in the front office during the interview, listening to our conversation. She introduced herself and asked if I could return to meet with her. I apologized to her for not being able to return due to prior commitments. However, we were able to schedule a second luncheon meeting a few weeks out for K.C, Barbara, Alma, and I.

After a couple of weeks, we met again. The luncheon went well. Alma and I decided that K.C and Barbara were the right employers we were looking for. They had great values and they value others, which made us feel very welcome and right at home. Alma was as excited for me as I was for her, and with our daughter starting college, this move was very important for us.

I would start work with KCB Builders in April 2015. I immediately started making phone calls and reconnecting with people I hadn't spoken to since the collapse of the economy.

I remember scheduling a meeting with one of my past clients at Division Three Concrete, and I introduced K.C to Greg. It turned out to be a profitable introduction. Since then, we have successfully accomplished several projects together.

*****

Over the next few years, we grew to about 200 plus employees, which was the record high for KCB. The office personnel also increased from three to seven people. I was now running ten foremen and about twelve projects at a time. This was something I was used to doing so it came fairly natural to me.

The projects were all different, some ranged from three hundred thousand up to one-million-dollar projects. While others ranged from one million up to eight-million-dollar projects. The formula to select which foreman was going to be running what project has been the same formula I've used for years.

"It's not about the right project for the foreman, it's about the right foreman for the project"

KC and Abidan at the 2018 Las Vegas - World Of Concrete

Chapter 17

New Contract

The hard work you put in when no one's looking, pays off in the long run.

After a few years of working at KCB, it was time for the renewal of my contract. Both KC and Barbara would schedule a meeting. However, this time they would also bring in Gary, the company's CPA / CFO. We all discussed the successes that KCB had accomplished in just a short span.

Gary asked me a series of questions.

"What are your future plans?"

"What are your salary expectations?"

"How can we be more profitable?" There were several others.

I calmly responded to his questions with some of my own which included my plans and commitment at KCB for the long haul, and added, "I'm also planning to start up a non-profit training facility to enhance the blue-collar workers' ability to perform at a higher and more productive level."

I then responded to the salary question. I was thorough with my explanation about what I was expecting in terms of a yearly salary, and my yearly bonus. A combined total of over $200K yearly.

I interjected that KCB could be more profitable if we could focus more on quality versus quantity. This would mean reducing our gross yearly revenue by a small percentage and in return, we would add many more successful projects that would display our quality approach.

KCB also put in place a PO system that helped with cost control and several other programs.

Once the meeting was over, Gary wanted me to know that if I had any future investments and/or ventures, to please consider calling him as he would be open to discussing and possibly partnering up.

I thanked everyone for the outcome of the meeting.

Later that month KCB renewed my three-year contract as agreed. I can honestly say that I am a very fortunate person, having met KC and Barbara.

World of Concrete Meet, Las Vegas

Annual Installation and Awards Banquet

Invitation & Challenge

Becoming a master at my craft has taken me over 24 years, and today I still have room for improvement. I will always welcome new ideas, mentors, teachers, and good old age wisdom.

I love to learn, and learning is listening. *Sometimes you just have to be quiet, pay attention, and keep notes.*

I enjoy helping people understand construction and its different approaches. Facilitating methods while arriving with quality is my main focus, and understanding that safety will take precedence over any schedule is part of what I like to instill in every employee.

We have evolved in our construction community and will continue to learn and grow *as long as we have a passion for what we love to do.* ***I invite and challenge you to come be with us in this exciting venture, to not only provide you with access to your dreams, but the wealth and good life that comes with it!***

If I can make it through this environment so can you. Don't give up on your dreams. Fight for what you believe in and continue to move towards your goals. Every day you move forward, you get closer!

~ Abidan Padilla

"You are the foundation of your own future."

The Padilla Family

In search of a new beginning and a great future.

Abidan Padilla's parents, Adelaida and Santiago, arrived in the USA in the late '60s, both from Michoacán, Mexico. Santiago worked the avocado farms in the '70s.

Abidan Padilla was born at Mission Hospital in Fallbrook California, on November 4, 1976. After Abidan was born his father decided it was time to move to the inner city for better job opportunities.

After arriving in downtown L.A., they discovered that having five kids made it improbable to be accepted by a potential landlord. So they were given the opportunity to live with close relatives for a short time, this worked out well.

His mother would not leave the apartment when his father would go out in search for daily jobs. It didn't take long. His father finally found a job, and after a few months, they would move into their own apartment in the city of Compton.

In 1980, his mother gave birth to Joanna, their youngest daughter, at the Martin Luther King hospital in Compton California.

Abidan grew up with his three brothers, and two sisters, Epimenio, Santiago Jr., Jose, Maria, and Joanna. Then in 1990 his parents adopted two younger cousins, Francisco Gutierrez and Graciela Esquivel.

His parents would continue to move a few more times throughout South Central L.A., Compton, and Watts, before settling in into what they were going to call home for the next decade; The Nickerson Gardens Housing projects.

Always onward.

Adelaida, Alma, Abidan, and Santiago Padilla, Sr.

New Personal Goals — Stephanie, Austin

Teaching others will be the best gift I can ever make.

Stephanie Padilla:

Ten years from now I will probably be a completely different person, and that is the beauty in life. We are all constantly growing mentally, spiritually, and emotionally, and with growth comes a lot of knowledge. Over the past years, I have seen both of my parents grow and flourish into such amazing role models. Knowing all the struggles they faced and overcame helped me see that we can all make something out of ourselves if we really set goals. I am very fortunate to have my parents, and although I do not come from the projects, like my parents, I have a lot of respect for those who do. There is beauty in the struggle, and I think people who realize that will flourish too.

Our mindsets play a big role in our outcomes of life, and thanks to my parents, my brother and I know we can achieve our goals. I hope to one day be a great parent just like my parents. Their journey is far from over, and I feel so blessed to be a part of it.

Family over everything.

Abidan Austin Padilla, Jr.:

I would like to start by thanking my parents for all their hard work over the past twenty years, and the sacrifices they made to secure a better life for me and my sister. My parents are my biggest role models, and they showed me that anything is possible. They raised me and my sister in the best way possible, and there are no words to describe the love I have for them. I would also like to thank God for putting me and my family in such a blessed position, especially knowing that my parents grew up in such a tough environment.

One of my major goals in life is to become a successful person spiritually and financially, and although it may be a journey, it will be worth it knowing that I will make my parents proud. Another one of my major ambitions is to live life happily and try to become a better person *each and every day.*

* * * * *

With Stephanie and Austin – Stephanie graduates from CUSB, while Austin starts college at the University of California, Riverside.

Ways to Turn Desires Into Gold

On November 18, 2007, I wrote the following:

1. I want to earn $250,000 to $300,000 yearly salary plus bonuses and set a goal that I would be a millionaire before I'm thirty-five years of age.
2. In return, I will give back to the Community Churches an amount of 10% of my earnings for charity purposes.
3. By November 4, 2011, I intend to possess the millions I desire.
4. I plan to assist the company for which I am currently working to the best of my abilities, making it successful, and shortly after branching out on my own.

Abidan Padilla 9:15 p.m.

My son Austin is here studying his A.B.C's; my daughter Stephanie is in her room reading the Bible, and my wife Alma is in the living room also reading.

I don't plan failure. I plan success.

Abidan's Personal Goals and Prayer

December 30, 2019   Personal Goals

Dear God,

It's been a little over twelve years since I last wrote to you my goals. My wife Alma has since become a manager with the school district; my daughter Stephanie just graduated from the University with her BA in Psychology; my son Austin is near graduating from High School and has recently been accepted to Cal Baptist University.

I continue to pursue my goals and dreams, currently working for "KCB." KC and Barbara are the owners who have treated my family and me with great appreciation for friendship, more than just a business relationship.

Our parents are getting older with some health concerns. I would like to thank you personally for hearing our prayers and getting them healthy again.

My wife and I recently started a couple of companies. The first is a non-profit 501 C3 with the purpose to assist the common person in life by providing skills and opportunities for success. The second is The Concrete Corporation, intended to generate income and assist the non-profit company with expenses.

I sincerely appreciate you, God, for everything you've done for this "World," from the air we breathe, the water we drink, the feeling of touch, the beautiful sights you allow us to see, listening to the sounds of nature, and so many tastes that you allow us to enjoy!

Thank you, my Lord, God.

Sincerely,

Your son,
Abidan Padilla

www.ingramcontent.com/pod-product-compliance
Lightning Source LLC
Chambersburg PA
CBHW071200090426
42736CB00012B/2402